Wild H

Contents

Wild Horses?

When you think of wild animals, do you think of tigers with big teeth? Or crocodiles hiding in dark rivers?

There is another wild animal you may not think of. It has a long neck, a flowing mane, and powerful legs. It's the horse!

3

Most horses work for people and are not wild. They pull wagons, run races, and help ranchers. Horses that live with and work for people are called domestic horses. Most horses today are domestic.

But some horses live on their own, away from people. They live the way all horses used to live. They are wild horses.

Horse History

Long, long ago, horses lived all over the earth.

One of the earliest horses was called *Eohippus*. *Eohippus* was about the size of a fox.

This is a cave painting of an early horse from about 17,000 years ago.

Between 8,000 and 10,000 years ago, horses disappeared from North America. No one knows why.

7

But horses still lived wild in other places.

Then, about 5,000 years ago, people began
to ride horses, and horses became domestic.

8

Spanish explorers brought horses back to North America about 500 years ago. They rode these horses as they explored the land.

Later, Native Americans and settlers used horses. It was much easier to travel and hunt on horseback than on foot.

Horses pulled covered wagons of pioneers across the country.

10

Over time, some horses got away. They
learned to live without people, the way horses
used to live. Today, wild horses still live in
many places.

11

How Wild Horses Live

Most wild horses in North America live in the deserts and mountains of the West.

Montana
North Dakota
Oregon
Idaho
Wyoming
Nevada
Utah
Colorado
California
Arizona
New Mexico

Sable Island
Assateague Island
Shackleford Island
Cumberland Island

Places wild horses live

12

The wild horses of Sable Island, Canada, may have swum ashore after a shipwreck many, many years ago.

Some wild horses live on islands.

Wild horses eat grasses and shrubs. Island horses also eat seaweed.

13

Wild horses live in groups called bands.

Bands are made up of one male
horse and several female horses.
The babies, called foals, are also
part of the band.

Horse Names

Male horse	Stallion
Female horse	Mare
Baby horse	Foal
Young female horse	Filly
Young male horse	Colt

14

Each band lives in its own area of land. The band protects its grasses from other animals.

Wild horses in the West are called mustangs. The word *mustang* comes from a Spanish word for stray.

How Wild Horses Survive

Life is hard for wild horses. Desert horses have to find grass and water on very dry land. Other wild horses have to dig through ice to find food in the winter.

Sable Island horses grow thick coats for the winter.

The average domestic horse lives 20–30 years. Few wild horses live more than 20 years.

Because life is hard for wild horses, they don't live as long as domestic horses.

17

wild horse

domestic horse

Wild horses don't grow as large as domestic horses. But this is helpful to wild horses because smaller horses need less food.

Wild horses have shorter, stronger legs than domestic horses. Wild horses run on rocky, uneven lands. If they fall, their strong legs might not break.

Wild horses are very, very strong. Horses love to run, and wild horses can run longer and farther than the strongest racehorses.

Protecting Wild Horses

In 1971, a law was passed to protect wild horses. This law said that no one can kill or capture a wild horse.

People take care of wild horses in many ways.
If there are too many horses and not enough
grass to eat, people move some horses to
other areas. People work to keep horse
bands together.

21

Horses in the Black Hills Sanctuary

Most of these horses live their entire lives in their new protected area. Other horses might be cared for until they can be adopted.

To many people, wild horses stand for strength and freedom. These horses live just as they did thousands of years ago, wild and free.

Index